PRAISE FOR *A SUIT OR A SUITCASE*

"These poems help me live. *A Suit or a Suitcase* explores intricate metaphysical subjects, the nature and interrelationships between the body, the mind, the soul, the self, mortality, and time, with a broad, companionable generosity. Her questions shed sparks, yet her lines, her images, are purposeful; they aspire to clarify rather than obfuscate. These poems share the fruits of a difficult aloneness, and the work of a polished mind and an endlessly revised self that has learned to endure mystery, even while lugging around 'the whole shebang' of her life, even while staying home, staying put. Smith's is a poetry of grace."
—Diane Seuss, Pulitzer Prize–winning author of *frank: sonnets* and *Modern Poetry*

"*A Suit or a Suitcase* is a confident, satisfying collection of poems. Not a word or idea is out of place. The title poem is a real standout."
—Roxane Gay, *New York Times* bestselling author of *Hunger* and *Bad Feminist*

"I love Maggie Smith's poems. She is immensely generous to all readers. She gives us her sometimes dark, often hilarious, always questioning, always familiar awareness of the strangeness of the everyday. She shares her insights, her pain, her humility, her intense love of people and the world. To read her poems is to become more aware, more sensitive, more loving, more present, more alive."

—Matthew Zapruder, author of
I Love Hearing Your Dreams and *Story of a Poem*

"The poems in *A Suit or a Suitcase* point us to larger considerations of the divine. Maggie Smith writes a poetry of profound belonging. The emotional wilderness we enter is rendered more sacred thanks to her commitment to a commonality of speech. At the core of her work is a playfulness, yet too, an insightfulness that urges self-reflection. This is a book to return to again and again. Why? One day we will find ourselves near a river and there will be Maggie proclaiming every version of who we are."

—Major Jackson, author of *Razzle Dazzle*

PRAISE FOR *DEAR WRITER*

"Like some seminal texts for writers by writers (Eudora Welty's *One Writer's Beginnings*, Virginia Woolf's *A Letter to a Young Poet*), this is at once pure craftmanship and a glimpse of the gut-wrenching, visceral ways great writers feel the world around them. A lovely invitation into Smith's processes that is luminous and shimmering, designed to make writing feel accessible yet magical!"

—*Library Journal* (starred review)

"Oh, how I wish I'd had access to this book thirty-five years ago, when I was just starting out as a writer! Maggie Smith has created an offering here of great substance and generosity—walking writers of all ages (and of all levels) through the sometimes wild and terrifying landscape of literary endeavor. With encouraging words, stories from her own life, and—best of all—exercises that are actually helpful, she lends a hand to all. I admire this book, and its author, with all my heart."

—Elizabeth Gilbert, #1 *New York Times* bestselling author of *Big Magic*

Praise for *You Could Make This Place Beautiful*

"This book is extraordinary."

—Ann Patchett

"This book is a gift."

—Leslie Jamison,
bestselling author of *The Empathy Exams*

"Maggie Smith's book is one of the most powerful memoirs I've ever read."

—Kwame Alexander, *Oprah Daily*

Praise for *Goldenrod*

"Maggie Smith is that rare poet who can inspire you, break your heart, and make you stop astonished at the planet around you—all in the same poem, often in the same moment."

—Ilya Kaminsky, author of *Deaf Republic*

"To read Maggie Smith is to embrace the achingly precious beauty of the present moment."

—*Time*

Praise for *Keep Moving*

"Smith['s] superpower as a writer: her ability to find the perfect concrete metaphor for inchoate human emotions and explore it with empathy and honesty."

—*Slate*

"*Keep Moving* speaks to you like an encouraging friend reminding you that you can feel and survive deep loss, sink into life's deep beauty, and constantly, constantly make yourself new."

—Glennon Doyle, #1 *New York Times* bestselling author of *Untamed*

Praise for *Good Bones*

"Truthful, tender, and unafraid of the dark, the poems in *Good Bones* are lyrically charged love letters to a world in desperate need of her generous eye."

—Ada Limón, former US poet laureate and author of *The Hurting Kind*

"Smith's poems affirm the virtues of humanity: compassion, empathy, and the ability to comfort one another when darkness falls."

—D. A. Powell, author of *Repast*

Also by Maggie Smith

Dear Writer: Pep Talks & Practical Advice for the Creative Life
The People's Project: Poems, Essays, and Art for Looking Forward
My Thoughts Have Wings
You Could Make This Place Beautiful
Goldenrod
Keep Moving: The Journal
Keep Moving: Notes on Loss, Creativity, and Change
Good Bones
The Well Speaks of Its Own Poison
Lamp of the Body

A SUIT
or
A SUITCASE

poems

Maggie Smith

**WASHINGTON
SQUARE PRESS**

ATRIA

NEW YORK   AMSTERDAM/ANTWERP   LONDON
TORONTO   SYDNEY/MELBOURNE   NEW DELHI

ATRIA

An Imprint of Simon & Schuster, LLC
1230 Avenue of the Americas
New York, NY 10020

For more than 100 years, Simon & Schuster has championed authors and the stories they create. By respecting the copyright of an author's intellectual property, you enable Simon & Schuster and the author to continue publishing exceptional books for years to come. We thank you for supporting the author's copyright by purchasing an authorized edition of this book.

No amount of this book may be reproduced or stored in any format, nor may it be uploaded to any website, database, language-learning model, or other repository, retrieval, or artificial intelligence system without express permission. All rights reserved. Inquiries may be directed to Simon & Schuster, 1230 Avenue of the Americas, New York, NY 10020 or permissions@simonandschuster.com.

Copyright © 2026 by Maggie Smith

"We're not our souls, we're not our bodies; we're the shimmering border between.": from *The Hero of This Book* by Elizabeth McCracken. Copyright © 2022 by Elizabeth McCracken. Used by permission of HarperCollins Publishers.

All rights reserved, including the right to reproduce this book or portions thereof in any form whatsoever. For information, address Atria Books Subsidiary Rights Department, 1230 Avenue of the Americas, New York, NY 10020.

First Washington Square Press/Atria Books hardcover edition March 2026

WASHINGTON SQUARE PRESS / ATRIA BOOKS and colophon are registered trademarks of Simon & Schuster, LLC

Simon & Schuster strongly believes in freedom of expression and stands against censorship in all its forms. For more information, visit BooksBelong.com.

For information about special discounts for bulk purchases, please contact Simon & Schuster Special Sales at 1-866-506-1949 or business@simonandschuster.com.

The Simon & Schuster Speakers Bureau can bring authors to your live event. For more information or to book an event, contact the Simon & Schuster Speakers Bureau at 1-866-248-3049 or visit our website at www.simonspeakers.com.

Interior design by Kyoko Watanabe

Manufactured in the United States of America

1 3 5 7 9 10 8 6 4 2

Library of Congress Control Number: 2025004846

ISBN 978-1-6680-9005-3
ISBN 978-1-6680-9006-0 (ebook)

 Let's stay in touch! Scan here to get book recommendations, exclusive offers, and more delivered to your inbox.

for the *me* of me
& the *you* of you

Contents

1. DETAIL

Detail	3
A Suit or a Suitcase	5
Rasp	8
Pastoral	10
The Score	12
Poem Beginning with a Line from *It's the Great Pumpkin, Charlie Brown*	14
Vision	16
In Geologic Time, It Happened Just Seconds Ago	18
Beside Myself	21

2. STUDY

Study	27
Window Seat	29
Foal	31

Now They're Saying Isolation Atrophies the Brain	33
Time-Stamped	35
Lula	37
Hope Chest	39
Doppelgänger	41
Poem Beginning with a Line from *An Exact Replica of a Figment of My Imagination*	43
Gatefold	45

3. SELF-PORTRAIT

Self-Portrait as an Incomplete List of Mysteries	49

4. TRIPTYCH

Triptych	59
Where	62
Genetic memory	65
For years I lived	67
New Year Sestina	69
Supermoon Haibun	72
Three Thoughts After Crossing Nameless Creek	73
The Before Picture	75

Document	77
Poem Beginning with a Text to My Neighbor	79

5. INSTALLATION

Installation	83
To Each Its Own	85
On the Occasion of My Feet Inexplicably Leaving the Ground	88
You Ask If I Believe in the Afterlife	90
Poem Beginning with a Mishearing	92
This human life	94
Homebody	96
Tercet	98
I call them back to me—	100

Acknowledgments	103
Credits	105

*My body is a lens
I can look through with my mind.*

—AMA CODJOE

*We're not our souls, we're not our bodies;
we're the shimmering border between.*

—ELIZABETH MCCRACKEN

*The body is living art. Your movement through
time and space is art. A painter has brushes.
You have your body.*

—ANNA HALPRIN

1.
DETAIL

Detail

You're the kind who looks at a painting
and wonders what's happening beyond

the stretched canvas, where it wraps
around the wood frame, as if
it were a detail from a larger work

or, like a photograph, one small scene
inside a wider one, curated by the eye.

You wonder what's beyond
the bowl of fruit, beyond the gray sea
with its meal of wrecked ships,

beyond the mother holding her burning,
red-cheeked child. You're the kind

who thinks there must be more
than this, more than what you see.
The kitchen might be filling with bees,

drawn buzzing to the bowl of red
and yellow apples. And the waves,

the waves might be ruffling white
and folding over on themselves—
breaking, breaking like a fever.

A Suit or a Suitcase

You ask what I'll miss about this life.
Everything but cruelty, I think.

But you want one specific thing,
so here—I'll miss my body. I'll miss

its companionship, how it's traveled
with me, never leaving me—& by *me*,

I mean my mind. My soul? My self?
I don't know what to call it, & besides,

my body hasn't traveled with me.
I've traveled inside it. Do I wear it

or does it carry me? Is the body a suit
or a suitcase? Bear with me here.

I've always thought of who I am
as being concentrated in my head & chest,

as if there's a waterline at my rib cage
& contrary to their density, thoughts

& feelings stay afloat. You asked
what I'll miss about this life, & now

I'm way down a rabbit hole, wondering
if I could breathe deeply enough

to redistribute my mind more evenly
throughout my body—or *soul* rather

than *mind*? Or *self*? I don't even know
what to call the *me* of me. I imagine

filling my body completely, filling it,
every inch, to the skin. Shh. Listen.

Ideas are whispering in my wrists
& all along the slopes of my calves.

When you lay your head on my thigh,
when you kiss the backs of my knees, listen.

I'm trying to tell you what I'll miss—
everything but cruelty, but mostly this.

Rasp

The heat rises in distorted gold
        waves around fire
               but without fire,
    shimmering, twisting

anything seen through it.
        The heat rises, rasping
               the air it rises through,
    scuffing the surface,

if the air has a surface.
        The tall summer
               field is the keeper
    of secrets. Lie down

and forget your body, forgive
>   your body its bad cradle,
>   its brokenness.
>   Lie down and listen

to the rasp, to heat sweep
>   the pale, dry grass as if
>   it were your own
>   breathing, as if the field

you've pressed your shape into
>   is a broom in reverse,
>   a broom being
>   swept by the wind.

Pastoral

The field is a document
I refuse to sign,
a contract with fine print
written in clover
so small, I can't tell
if arbitration is required
or if I can sue this vast
green for not living
up to some pastoral
ideal. Where does it say
the field must make
a reasonable effort to be
soft under my feet?
Dry leaves are beginning
to startle the pavement.
One scuffs along,
curled like a hand

cramped around something

for so long, it can't open.

Oh illegible clover.

I'm putting away

my good signing pen.

The Score

Sometimes I feel like I'm writing the score
for a film that doesn't yet exist,

but everything that will happen
in the film will happen to me.

Is this what they call plot? This daily
picking up of the same things—

glasses, coffee cup, pen, book, keys—
and setting them back down again?

Narrative has always troubled me,
so I'll leave that to someone else

and write the mood instead, also
approximating setting: a little piano

to suggest rain, and violin for a river,
long and thin. That key change?

A meander. If the score is plain
and sweet, it's because the life is—

mostly. I don't know how it ends,
but given the budget, it will end quietly.

One day I'll find myself near a river,
and I'll realize, *This is that film,*

*the one I scored, and this is the scene where
rain starts falling.* And in that moment

it will, and it will sound like piano.

Poem Beginning with a Line from *It's the Great Pumpkin, Charlie Brown*

Just look—nothing but sincerity
as far as the eye can see—
the way the changed leaves,

flapping their yellow underbellies
in the wind, glitter. The tree
looks sequined wherever

the sun touches. Does anyone
not see it? Driving by a field
of spray-painted sheep, I think

the world is not all changed.
The air still ruffles wool
the way a mother's hand

busies itself lovingly in the hair
of her small boy. The sun
lifts itself up, grows heavy

treading there, then lets itself
off the hook. Just look at it
leaving—the sky a tigereye

banded five kinds of gold
and bronze—and the sequin tree
shaking its spangles like a girl

on the high school drill team,
nothing but sincerity. It glitters
whether we're looking or not.

Vision

In the last minutes
      before sleep, I close

           one eye at a time,
      shifting everything

just slightly. I can lie
      still and watch

           the doorway,
      the dresser, the framed

paint-by-number
      inch over,

           inch back.
      I'm not moving

anything, only marveling
    that each eye,

        so close to
    the other,

has its own view.

In Geologic Time, It Happened Just Seconds Ago

Our honeymoon was a strand
        of scenic overlooks. I first wrote
                strange—a *strange* of scenic

overlooks—my mistake, and strange
        enough was the desert penned
                in red ink. The scene

was either Sedona or Mars. They say
        the iron in the rocks calls
                to the iron in our blood,

so it tugs on us. It tugged. We stayed
        on Airport Mesa, where we called
                the crowds drawn to sanguine

sunsets "tourists," as if we weren't,
    and where, each night, the Milky Way
        made a mess of the sky.

Was I the only one who wanted
    to wipe its white smudge away,
        to polish the night

black again? Our honeymoon
    was a stranded scene I overlooked.
        We posed for photographs

we never took. I remember the moon
    framed above the landscape, looking
        silvery as a tintype

taken in a modern-day ghost town.
    The last day, we reached the canyon
        and saw where the river

had over millions of years chewed it down
    to bone, clear to the canyon's
        strange marrow, riven

into red, copper, and purple—bands
    like sunsets compressed and recorded
        in rock. That view

remains. Our honeymoon was a strand,
    a strangeness, a look ahead. I wrote
        only what I could see.

Beside Myself

The energy worker tells me
I'm not inside my body.
"Then where am I?"
She gestures to the left of me:
"You're here."

I've been crayoned outside
the lines, I think. Or picture
a body casting a shadow:
that's the *me* of me,
the shadow my body
throws down beside me.

"I was beside myself,"
we say when stunned,
when shock electrifies

until our hair's on end,
our eyes are wide & unseeing,
& we're hovering just beyond
the body's reach.

"How do I get back
inside myself?" I ask.
She sits in front of me,
knees kissing mine.
"Picture a flame inside you."
I do, & I inhale to pull
the flame higher, to grow it
larger, larger, until it fills me.
Until I'm flush
with myself, one whole person.
Complete as a breakfast, I think.

With each breath I'm pulling
myself together. Cinching
the threads. Oh little shadow,
falling away from me,
come back. Oh self,
crayoned outside the frame,
come back, come back.

She looks at me.
Softens her gaze.
Looks again.
"Oh, there you are."

2.
STUDY

Study

I'm beginning to suspect this life
is a study for another one,

research for a larger project
still taking shape. I don't mean

heaven, no. If these days
are notes that will serve me later,

I'm taking copious notes.
If this world is not the real world—

I mean, not the final version—
will the real world at least

resemble this draft? I'm beginning
to suspect this life is practice,

and what of these practice
children—are they mine

to keep? What can I carry
forward except these reminders?

Each day is a note I jot down
under the day before.

Window Seat

It feels like withholding, like punishment—
where there should be a small oval of light,

only smooth beige plastic, my view
rescinded, given instead to the woman ahead

& the woman behind. I'm no stranger
to small deprivations. For a year I kept

myself like a flame, cupping my hand
around my wavering life whenever

the wind picked up, looking nowhere
but in—where else, alone, to look?

There was no window, no sky, no clouds
above or below, no kiss between

my shoulder blades, no rivers, no fingers,
no rows of white houses below, no rows

of white teeth on my thigh, no cloud-shade
laid upon fields, no hand gripping

my hip bone, no mountains, no lakes,
no mouth with me inside it. I looked

in & in & in, no view or body assigned me
but my own. No sweat, no throat,

no waves from this height.
No window, no clouds, no light.

Foal

Now that I have no other heart
to which I might apply my own,
I polish my mind and polish
and polish until its tarnish
comes off black on a soft cloth.
My god, it's filthy.
There must be more
gleam, I think, and I sleep
so little for seeking it.

Now that I have no other body
to which I might apply my own,
I'm learning to use my body
in new ways, ways I can use it
alone. I run new-foal-like
through the neighborhood,
then laugh, doubled over, rosy-

exhausted when I'm done.
I didn't know my body
could do that. If I said
I feel newer now, glistening
like a just-born horse—
and as awkward, as startled—
could you see it?
I mean, just look at me.

Now that I have no other mind
to which I might apply my own,
I polish it to near-shining.
Thoughts come away
cleaner and cleaner.
If I lean in close enough,
I can see my reflection.

Now They're Saying Isolation Atrophies the Brain

Talking to yourself in an empty room
sometimes feels like prayer but isn't.

It isn't prayer if you're not asking
for anything, and what would you ask for?

Any request more specific than *save me*
would be so granular as to be worthless.

It can't be prayer if you're standing
at your kitchen counter, wearing an apron

and a far-off look. It can't be prayer
if you're walking in your neighborhood,

muttering to yourself, while Orion
keeps buckling and unbuckling his belt

over the houses. It can't be prayer if you have
the expectation of privacy. If you think

no one's listening. As a child I believed
so fiercely in the power of my own mind,

when I thought *apple*, I half expected
a real one, large and red, to appear

in my hand. Now I know better. I talk
to myself. Sometimes I even answer.

Time-Stamped

There is a revision of me that lives
in the future, watching me from the future,

which makes me a prototype,
an earlier version, the one she thinks of now.

She looks back at me and at the life
I live in the house she must think of

as *the old house*, and at my children—
her children—still lap-small

and sticky-cheeked. She watches us
the way I watch old, time-stamped versions

of myself, the roughest drafts, feeling
I'd slit a stranger's throat for the clean slate

that was mine—the slate I wanted
only to write and write on.

She watches from the future
to remind me I am not finished,

not as fleshed out as I feel.
I must be full of blanks she'll know

how to fill, and she'll fill them.
She looks back at me, and someone

looks back at her, and I am watching
every version of myself behind me:

never overridden or replaced
but saved, each of us saved.

Lula

We've been at this for years.
So long, it's a kind of marriage.
Why not believe the shadow

feels affection for the flesh?
That it longs to be bodied, that it dreams
of all it could do for me?

Sometimes I imagine handing it
a bag of groceries from the trunk
and sending it into the house.

We've been at this so long,
it's grown on me. It grows,
blurry doppelgänger

so nondescript, it's hard to know
even close-up—all outline, nothing
inside. What is a shadow

if not vestigial? A partner only
in a certain light? I've thought
about calling it Lula, the name

I'd been saving for another
child but will never need.
We've been at this long enough—

so long, it feels like marriage.
We touch without touch,
take turns outgrowing one another.

Hope Chest

As a bride, given
      away. Then again,

as a wife. Twice taken
      off a man's hands.

As a bride, presented
      as a gift. As a wife,

discarded. Not returned,
      not given back, but

disowned, buck passed.
      Not *doe a deer*

but the kind you pocket
      and spend. Or waste.

My dowry was the dear
    I am, the hope

chest I am, the whole
    of me folded inside

in lieu of linen and lace
    and the good silver,

so now I take it back. Dearly
    I take myself back.

Doppelgänger

Everyone has a twin somewhere. Like a child
given up at birth, I look for my features

wherever I go. Doppelgänger, I know
the luck you bring, but I can't stop

seeking you out. Other self, I want to project
myself to where you are. I want to trace

your shape with my finger, but you won't
feel me ruffling your hair. You won't

look at me. You only echo my movements,
a sleepwalker. Other doer, with you around,

everything is slightly off, like when Dylan
went electric. The hours are striped

with light as yellow as old newspapers;
the moon is grainier than an obit photo.

Not quite a door, I stand ajar. I'm two
places at once. I'm watching a movie,

but the person playing me isn't acting.
Double walker, you're not so bad.

You don't have red eyes and a black,
V-shaped unibrow like most evil twins.

But you won't look my way. You speak
but not to me. Your voice, which is mine,

crackles like a phone call from another country.

**Poem Beginning with a Line from *An Exact Replica
of a Figment of My Imagination***

*This is the happiest story
in the world with the saddest ending*

is the best you can hope for
if you have a good life, a good life

you've had for years, maybe
even decades, but you can't keep it.

Can a story, even the happiest,
be a happy story if the ending

is the saddest or even just
garden-variety, mid-level sad?

You know a rhetorical question
when you hear one.

Everything you think you own
is only lent you, then repo'd

all at once or taken piece
by piece. What makes the ending

so sad is the happiness
that precedes it. The happiest

story with the saddest
ending is textbook tragedy,

and it's your life, if you're lucky.

Gatefold

See how I've opened how
I've widened beyond

the frame I can't even see
the lines the not-quite

perforations where I should
collapse one panel into

another See this
expansion this expanse

my impression of a gatefold
as if I've pulled my ribs

apart   parted myself
and now   there is no way

to get the full   story back
into the small   and yes

tattered book   of the self

3.

SELF-PORTRAIT

Self-Portrait as an Incomplete List of Mysteries

How some days I feel time expanding, opening, the folds of its paper accordion pulling apart.

How once, hundreds of miles away from home, high on a mountaintop, I woke in the middle of the night and knew I needed to leave immediately. How, while I was sleeping, my daughter called me home.

Why our brains commit certain details to memory, holding tight, white-knuckled, but let others go.

How a poem becomes. Often, when one arrives, it feels like something I'm watching happen, not something I'm making happen.

Who I might be if I'd moved away from my hometown. I'd be someone different, I suspect, but I don't know who.

How the people we love can become strangers to us. *Estranged*, from the Latin *extraneare*, to treat as a stranger. And how strangers can become people we love.

How a poem is both the born creature and the birth record.

Who to hand these things to—these thoughts that accumulate each day like stones in my pockets. Whose palm to drop them into.

How some mornings my children look older than they did the night before. It's the shape of their faces, the roundness inexplicably giving way to hollows overnight, like moons waning.

How I'm the same person I was at seven, at seventeen, at twenty-seven, at thirty-seven, and now, and how I'm not the same at all, not copy-pasted year to year to year.

What rodeo I'm on. I've lost track of my rodeos.

How some things that are true do not stay true. The trueness wears off, like gold plating.

How we are supposed to live with—endure, tolerate—so many unanswered questions, each *why* a door down a long corridor that stretches, nightmarishly distorting, before our eyes.

What I am to the poem if not its parent.

How some days I feel time closing so tightly around me, I can't take a full breath.

How language is one moment gold, one moment tin. Then precious again. Then cheap, insufficient.

How a memory of a place changes the place, the mental topography distorting, seas evaporating, forest flattening to plain.

Who I might be if I had married someone else or not married at all. Who I might be a mother to.

How the poems trust me enough to keep arriving, and when a new one will knock at the door.

Why I can't remember some of the most harrowing moments. In a cop drama, this would be the "security tapes were erased" part of the show.

How to forgive myself for what I finally recognize was a pattern of cowardice. The pattern was so well-made, it aligned as it repeated, so the seams never showed.

How each poem rearranges me. I am different before, then during, then after. The ongoing after. The perpetual after.

How what was true then—read *then* as broadly as you want to—is no longer true now, but that does not mean it was a lie.

How, if a necklace was gold once but is tarnished now, nearly black, you still call it a gold necklace.

How my children found the door of me and opened it, entering the world. If they knocked elsewhere first but were not let inside, or if I was the first door they tried.

Why I wrote in a notebook at twenty-two, *I want to get my life to a pure point and stop.*

What *pure* meant to me then. What *stop* meant.

Why our souls are housed in these containers that rot, and why we haven't yet inherited—evolved into—a more durable design.

How to dial into the right idea at the right time, when in my mind it's like all of the radio stations are trying to come in at once. Hence: static.

What my children will remember of me. What will cling like burrs in them.

How writing about an experience, inscribing it, reinscribes the memory. How language constantly revises the mind.

How the alchemy of language is impossible to faithfully replicate again and again and again.

Why a desire to believe never grew into belief. The spell, the incantation, must have been missing some critical element.

Where I went, when I vanished from my own life. Where I had been, when I reappeared, rabbit from a hat, dove from a sleeve.

Where I might live if not here, and what the view from my window might be: toothy mountains, or a thick forest of fir trees, or a canyon the color of rust.

How, even in a firing kiln of a time, the mind does not grow brittle. It will not crack or break. Will not craze.

How I've lived so many lives inside this one body—*reincarnation light*—and how many I have left here.

Who I might be if my children had chosen another door, or no door at all.

Who I might be if the poems had not arrived.

How I could have been anyone, but I am this.

How the mind stays so supple. It gives, just a little, when I press.

4.
TRIPTYCH

Triptych

It takes you a minute to see
    they are not prints
        of the same painting

but three panels, subtly
    different, ocean waves
        that could be

storm clouds, just enough
    abstraction & movement,
        the sea's feral sadness.

It's wild & doesn't know
    how to settle or trust.
        Light sets each sequin

individually, & the waves
    wait to be chosen or
        passed over.

Who can blame the ones
    that fester? It has been
        an eternity, no end

in sight. In all three panels,
    you see the waves pleading
        before they fold

in on themselves, before
    they throw themselves
        blue, green, gray

at the shore, before the slap
    & sizzle of dissolving,
        all foam & gristle.

Three portraits of the sea
        like three photographs
               snapped seconds

apart. You know grief
        when you see it. No two
               waves break the same.

Where

When I think of her, the first person
I had to keep loving beyond her life,

beyond her body, the first person
I needed not to leave—

and when I think of the questions
I didn't ask her, so many questions,

because by the time I'd thought
to bring them and lay them

in her soft lap, she was gone—
for all intents and purposes, gone—

I still wonder if she was in there
somewhere, unanswering,

unanswerable. What haunts me
is not where she is now—scattered,

as she was in places dear to her—
but where *was* she? Where

did she go, and did she know
we were with her, that we belonged to her,

were *of* her? She was already scattered
inside herself, bits windblown

to the mind's far corners, beyond
knowing, beyond the borders

of that unmapped country—
but no, I remind myself,

and this is the only thought
that gives me peace:

If a country is unmapped,
it has no borders.

Genetic memory

explains how well I tread water.
How I can pull myself from the metaphor
of Pearl Harbor, declared dead,
and show up weeks later to tell you
I'm alive, I love you. How I know,
instinctively, where the cash-filled
coffee cans are buried, where the dogs
are buried. Where to find a drunk
when he doesn't come home for supper.
I know my way around a lumberyard,
an Elks lodge, a boardinghouse.
I know how to bang a door down
with the side of my fist, shouting a name
that doesn't need to be my father's
mother's father's. It could be any name.
The door doesn't have to be a door.
It's in my blood to have my jewelry

stolen off a cruise ship, my lover's
brake lines cut. I can climb
a telephone pole, shoe a horse,
pray to saints, load a gun. I remember
how to do what I haven't done.

For years I lived

as if my life were made of clay
or wood or even stone,
and all I had to do—"all"—
was mold or whittle or chisel
to change its shape. As if my life
were calling out from inside
a larger hunk of raw material,
of potential living. As if
the shape existed, and my work
was to reveal it. For years
I lived like that. Imagine
the absurdity of taking a chisel
to water, or trying
to sculpt it with your hands.
This is what a life is: water.
The work is letting it fill
the spaces it runs to; letting it

flow around or through the rest.
Yes, it glistens as silver
as a blade, and yes, it can drill
through stone, but it's soft
to the touch. A life does
what water does: It goes.

New Year Sestina

*The new year doesn't feel new
at all,* said my child,
the one who saw—who *sees*—
everything slant. *So what
if the world's a year older?
It's like when you turn*

seven but still feel six. Turning
one page doesn't make a book new.
Like that. I mean the old
year's still around, ghostchild
yanking at my sleeve. But what
does it want? To be seen,

to levitate our chairs? Now, see,
it's fucking with me. It turned
and I waited to feel—what?
Changed? Somehow new
myself? Even my child
at seven years old

wondered when the old
year would tire of us and see
itself out. That ghostchild
was an amateur haunt, turning
all the lights on. The news
sifted down, confetti. What

scheduled glitter, what
scheduled joy. My oldest
was right: the year's never new
enough. And not alone. See,
last year returns
as shadow: shadowchild,

shadowyear, yearchild.
It walks our halls for what?
Last year had its turn
but wants another—that old
story. It wants us to see
what we're missing. What's new?

But I've turned ghost enough, old
enough. Even my child sees
years for what they aren't: new.

Supermoon Haibun

Tonight the moon is all the weatherman can talk about. *Full Wolf Moon*, he calls it. *Old Moon, Snow Moon, Moon After Yule.* This is the closest the moon will be to us all year—*Perigee*, he says—but on the screen it looks like any other night. *Old Moon* is right. The eleven o'clock anchor in her red wrap dress thanks viewers for sharing their photos: *Thanks Kevin from Grove City for this gem!* It's a white blur over a suburban street. The weatherman goes in for a close-up: a bigger blur. I don't see what they see. No wolves here tonight, no howling, only a small dog whining to be let out. I open the back door, and she bolts into what should be darkness.

Outside, it's so bright
I laugh to see her shadow
pissing on the snow.

Three Thoughts After Crossing Nameless Creek

1.

The student who told you
her mother didn't name her for days.
For more than a week, everyone
called her *Baby*.

2.

Your daughter, when she first saw
the labeled world: *For sale. Open. Stop.*
Even *Hell Is Real*. It was love-
hate, reading being automatic.
Seeing a thing and
—immediately, without consent—
knowing it.

3.

Once, as a child, you tried to imagine
nothing—tried like hell to empty
your mind's shameful hoard.
But each time you had it,
you labeled it—*nothing*—
and that was something,
and you had to start again.

The Before Picture

It's complicated, my relationship status
with progress. I often prefer

the "before" picture. The future
is where I'm going only because

I have no choice, because time
moves in one direction, dragging

a bit of itself behind like meat.
An unseen hand keeps

tugging it—time's rabbit leg,
time's hunk of red venison—

just out of reach. Did I just describe
the future as bait? Am I strung

along? I know, when I arrive there,
it won't be there. Won't be *that*.

It'll be *now*, the way it is
right now. And again. Refresh,

refresh, refresh. The befores
pile up behind me. It's now again.

Document

The day is winter bright. I blink against it.
Each time the sun glints in my eyes,
each time I close my lids & let them go

orange & freckled with light,
my mind files it into a folder
that contains every other time

it's happened before: folders nested
inside folders going back, I imagine,
to one morning standing in my crib,

waiting for my mother to reach down
& lift me out, the sun keeping me
company until her arms appeared.

In the file: sun, sun_2, sun_3,
sun_75, sun_700. Each a document
I can return to & open, even revising

old experience with new thinking.
As if the eye has its own memory—
not *the mind's eye* but *the eye's mind*—

cataloging material it claims as its own.
Cataloging as long as I live: sun_7000,
sun_final, sun_final_revised, sun_final_final.

Poem Beginning with a Text to My Neighbor

I have an odd favor to ask: on windy nights,
if you don't mind, would you bring in
your wind chimes? They're right outside
my window, & I'm a light sleeper. It sounds

like someone ringing a small silver bell
again & again, expecting service. A maid. A butler.
They keep me up. Chime me up. Each time
I woke last night, half dreaming, I thought,

Is that the sound snow makes? I thought it was
ringing outside my small silver window,
against & against, expectant. Each time
I rang awake, I had to relearn the sound & where

it came from. Right outside my mind. At night,
at last. Please, I'm not a sleeper. I'm a light.

5.

INSTALLATION

Installation

When you leave the museum
of contemporary art, opening
the doors to midday, you may need
a few minutes to reset context:
the bike shackled to the sign
is only a bike, the sign only a sign,
no small white exhibit labels.
Out here birds are nothing
but their crumb-begging selves,
shitting on cars and waking us
before our alarms. Cars are cars,
shit is shit. You walk by some café
where a woman sits alone unless
you count the two dachshunds
eating torn bits of French bread
she's tossed under the table.
Aren't the dogs perfectly

curated and aren't the branches
like bicycle spokes, the noontime light
a playing card whirring between them?
As if sunlight as sunlight isn't
art enough, as if trees need to be
more than themselves to deserve
attention, which is a kind of love.
You're a stranger in this city,
finding your way to the hotel
where you'll sleep only tonight,
though when you arrive
you'll text someone, *I'm home.*
It's more than enough: the city
as itself and you as you inside it,
and home as home, et cetera, forever.

To Each Its Own

It feels right to me now,
to have ridden the pain here,
to have dismounted it
carefully, slowly,
because it is broad and tall,
because it is stomping its hooves,
because its eyes are wild, its breath hot,
and because it could rear up kicking
or bolt as I slide down its side,
my feet desperate for the ground.

My son can't see it, can't hear it.
He is dribbling his soccer ball
in the still-damp grass as he waits
for his friend, and I'm brought to tears

seeing him run, nothing—
nothing—chasing him.
The pain I rode to this place
seems not to know he is here.
I have to keep its eyes on me.
I think, *It makes one move*
toward that boy and—

But no, this pain is mine. And loyal.
My son will have his own.
May it be smaller, tamer
than this one. May it know mercy.
May it prick its ears
when it hears him cry.
May its eyes go gentle
when it senses it's bitten

too hard. If it knocks him down,
may it nuzzle him, nudge him
softly but urgently, as if to say,
Get up, I'm sorry, I didn't mean it.
I love you, I'm yours, get up.

On the Occasion of My Feet Inexplicably Leaving the Ground

Thing is, I've been lugging around my life,
the whole shebang, for years now—
the children, the dog, the hundred-year-old house
sloughing off around us, shingles peeling,
black mold blistering the basement cinder block,
one rat frozen open-mouthed in the backyard
trap, then two, then five, dog shit mysteriously
on my sock, from where, who knows,
my body and its own deferred maintenance,
the umpteen kinds of work I cobble together
to keep us standing and sound, to keep the house
standing and sound, my friends, my blood
attachments, two different therapists paid
out of pocket, plumbers and electricians

and veterinarians and pharmacists and pest
controllers paid out of pocket, the accounts
I check daily, grafting from one to cover
the other, never enough skin. I've got it all
strapped to my back and I never put it down,
not even to sleep, because who would I hand it
off to, and who's sleeping these days anyway,
even loaded up with melatonin and magnesium
and lemon balm, and hell, the weight
should pin me to the ground, but look! I can't
explain it, but my life is rising into the air.
It's lifting me. My life is rising and taking me with it.

You Ask If I Believe in the Afterlife

I don't. But what if I'm wrong, you say.
What if there's something else. What if
there's not one but multiple heavens.
What if each of us goes into our own dream.
What would I want the afterlife to be,
if I'm wrong. That's easy: I'd think
any song and it would start playing
inside me. Then another, and another,
and another. I'd be sitting under a tree,
sunlight filtering down through the leaves,
ringing against my skin. On second thought,
I don't think I'd have skin. I can't imagine
why I'd need a body at all in the afterlife.
What a relief, the idea of continuing

beyond the body. Outgrowing it,
like a childhood dress. If I'm wrong
about the afterlife, I say, I'd want to be
a sun-dappled stereo. My own mind
playing song after song, a hell of a score.

Poem Beginning with a Mishearing

The earth is a bowl of blood,
I think I hear the minister say.
A bowl of blood, heavy & warm,

not *full of love.* Stained glass
made the light work so hard
to get inside—sun & pane

a kind of marriage.
I remember my daughter
asking once, *What is the earth*

for? What could I do
but gesture at everything
around us, sweeping my arms

wide: *For this, to be full of this.*
To be home, where I am tonight,
the children in their beds,

heavy with sleep, heavy & warm
& my best guess—what can I do
but guess?—at what the earth is for.

This human life

must look so small, undetectable even,
from the vantage point where I imagine

a god could see me, and I do sometimes
imagine a god like a sentient star

out beyond where our instruments
could find it, then I talk myself

out of the image. Out of the concept
entirely. From a distance, I know

I'm an ant tunneling my way
through sand between plastic panels,

watched—or not—from outside.
My puny movements on this planet,

all the things I've done or built
with my own body or mind, seem

like nothing at all. But from the inside
this life feels enormous, unlimited

by the self—by *selfness*—
vaster even than the sparkling

dark it can't be seen from.

Homebody

Meaning staying in one place.
Meaning staying in one's place.
How *constant* almost rhymes
with *constraint*. How with fewer
variables, I become one.
Driving around my hometown
is a game of   *that used to be a*
               that used to be a
My children were born in the same
hospital   as I was
             as my mother was
Thirty years apart we were buzzed
through the same ward doors
and we emptied ourselves there.
But I am so full. Meaning staying
in oneself. Meaning staying
in one's body. I am full of this

place—home, and its used-to-be-
banks, used-to-be-diners. I see
myself change against the backdrop.
Two nights ago I dreamt a river
cut me off from someplace—
where? I couldn't leap from one
bank to the other, couldn't bear
the cold current. Then all at once
my dream-self settled. Thought,
Nothing to it. Meaning staying.

Tercet

for V & R

There's a world in which none
of the worst of what happened
happened. We live in a different house

on a different tree-lined street.
Maybe our names are changed,
maybe even our faces. Our hearts

get broken there, too—
there's no world without that—
but not like here. The other

world has other devils—
there's no world without them—
but the ones we know too well here

are strangers there. They don't
recognize our changed faces.
They can't call our new names.

There's a world in which we can live
unaware of what happened
in this one. Unable even

to imagine it. But wherever we are,
we are—the me of me & the you
of each of you. The tercet of us

I swear there can be no world without.

I call them back to me—

flimsy selves of the past,
some vellum-thin, clearly

unfinished. Not fleshed out,
not fully—only children

really, stopped in time, still
tottering about in their

mother's high heels,
meaning mine?

I didn't know them,
their little plots forgotten

just as they began
to rise. I didn't know

what any of them,
any of *us*, would become

in the end, which is not yet
where we are.

I call them back.
I'm ready, I tell them.

I think I know now
where we're going, all of us,

together. I think I know
where the story is going.

Come back, come back,
I can finish it.

Acknowledgments

To my literary agent, Joy Tutela: Thank you. I'm so grateful for—and in awe of—what you've made possible in my life.

To my editor at Washington Square Press, Jenny Xu: Having your eyes and mind on these pages was a privilege and a joy. Thank you.

To Libby McGuire, Holly Rice, Maudee Genao, Joanna Pinsker, Dayna Johnson, James Iacobelli, Ifeoma Anyoku, and everyone at Atria: Thank you. You all make so much magic happen.

To Anya Backlund, Cale Zepernick, Rebecca Rhodes, Miyako Hannan-Scarponi, and everyone at Blue Flower Arts: Thank you for helping me take this show on the road, and for taking such good care of me.

To the poet Catherine Pierce, who has been my dear friend and first reader for more than twenty-five years now: Thank you, Katie. You make me better.

And to Violet and Rhett, two-thirds of the trinamic trio: I love you more.

Credits

Thanks to the editors of the following journals in which the following poems first appeared, sometimes in slightly different versions or with different titles:

The Adroit Journal: "Now They're Saying Isolation Atrophies the Brain" & "You Ask If I Believe in the Afterlife"

Alaska Quarterly Review: "Poem Beginning with a Text to My Neighbor" & "To Each Its Own"

The American Poetry Review: "Hope Chest," "On the Occasion of My Feet Inexplicably Leaving the Ground," "The Score," & "Where"

The Baffler: "Installation"

Berfrois: "Homebody" & "Triptych"

The Bitter Southerner: "I call them back to me—"

EPOCH: "Poem Beginning with a Mishearing" (as "At the Wedding")

Los Angeles Review: "New Year Sestina"

Mother Tongue: "Self-Portrait as an Incomplete List of Mysteries"

The Nation: "A Suit or a Suitcase"

A New Decameron: "Genetic memory"

Ninth Letter: "Poem Beginning with a Line from *An Exact Replica of a Figment of My Imagination*"

Numéro Cinq: "Study"

Open Letters Monthly: "Doppelgänger"

Poem-a-Day (Academy of American Poets): "Rasp" & "This human life"

Poetry International: "Vision"

Provincetown Arts: "Pastoral"

The Shanghai Literary Review: "Window Seat"

Sidereal: "Time-Stamped"

The Southern Review: "Poem Beginning with a Line from *It's the Great Pumpkin, Charlie Brown*," "Supermoon Haibun," & "Tercet"

Tab Journal: "Gatefold"

Tinderbox: "Lula"

Willow Springs: "Three Thoughts After Crossing Nameless Creek"

Thank you to Mary Jo Salter for selecting "Hope Chest" for *The Best American Poetry 2024*.

"Poem Beginning with a Line from *An Exact Replica of a Figment of My Imagination*" borrows a line from Elizabeth McCracken's beautiful memoir.

"Poem Beginning with a Line from *It's the Great Pumpkin, Charlie Brown*" borrows a line of Linus's dialogue from the animated special by Charles Schulz.

About the Author

Maggie Smith is the award-winning, *New York Times* bestselling author of nine books of poetry and prose, including *Dear Writer: Pep Talks & Practical Advice for the Creative Life*; *My Thoughts Have Wings*; *You Could Make This Place Beautiful*; *Goldenrod*; *Keep Moving: Notes on Loss, Creativity, and Change*; and *Good Bones*. A 2011 recipient of a Creative Writing Fellowship from the National Endowment for the Arts, Smith has also received a Pushcart Prize and numerous grants and awards from the Academy of American Poets, the Sustainable Arts Foundation, the Ohio Arts Council, the Greater Columbus Arts Council, and the Virginia Center for the Creative Arts. She has been widely published, appearing in *The New York Times*, *The Nation*, *The New Yorker*, *The Paris Review*, *The Atlantic*, *The Best American Poetry*, and more. You can follow her on social media @MaggieSmithPoet.